Dance On!

Written by Kerrie Shanahan

Illustrated by Nathalie Ortega

Flying Start
to Literacy®

T0363497

Contents

Chapter 1

Tessa's solo

Tessa and her dance class went through their routine one more time.

"Our performance is only six weeks from today." Miss Mia, their dance teacher, was stressed. "Now, let's get it right this time," she urged. "From the top – and one, two. A one, two, three."

The music started and the dancers sprang into action. They moved effortlessly and lightly. Tessa's heart raced a little faster as her solo approached.

This is what you've worked for all year, she thought.

As the spotlight shone on Tessa, she leapt gracefully into centre stage. She concentrated and smiled as she turned in the air.

And then she landed . . . but something wasn't right.

"Ahhhh!" she screamed.

An intense pain sliced through Tessa's right ankle.

"My ankle! My ankle!" Tessa cried.

Miss Mia and the other dancers ran to help her.

Then, everything happened so fast. She remembered her mother rushing to her side. She remembered being driven to the hospital. She remembered the pain. She remembered X-rays were taken. But, her most vivid memory was hearing the doctor's words.

"The good news is there's no break," he explained. "But the bad news is your ankle is badly sprained, so you'll have to stay off it for at least three weeks."

"What about my dance concert?" asked Tessa. "I'm performing my solo in six weeks' time."

"You should be fine by then," said the doctor, positively. "As long as your ankle heals as expected."

Tessa tried to smile, but she couldn't hold back the hot tears that welled up and forced their way down her cheeks. Her ankle hurt so much! How could she possibly be ready for the concert?

Why me? she thought.

Chapter 2

Cheering up Tessa

The next day, Tessa was still upset about her ankle.

"It's not fair," she complained.

"Cheer up," said Tessa's mother. "It's not the end of the world. You'll be back at school next week and you'll be dancing again before you know it."

"You don't understand." Tessa pouted. How could anyone possibly know how she was feeling? She had worked so hard and now, well, she didn't know if she would get to do her solo. She didn't even know if she would dance in the concert at all.

"Let's have some ice cream." Tessa's mum tried to get Tessa's mind off her problem. "Or I could make pancakes? Would you like to watch a movie or play Scrabble?"

But nothing that her mum suggested worked.

"I just want to be left alone," said Tessa, grumpily.

"Fine." Tessa's mum was losing patience, but then she had an idea. She knew exactly what Tessa needed. She jumped to her feet and disappeared upstairs.

Ten minutes later, Tessa's mother reappeared.

"Here." She handed Tessa a dusty box. "This might help you to feel better about *your* problem."

"What is it?" Tessa frowned.

"It belonged to your grandma. She wanted me to give it to you when you were old enough to understand. I think now is the perfect time."

Tessa could see her mother was sad. Tessa's grandma died two years ago and it still hurt to think about her.

Tessa brushed off the dust and ran her fingers over the lid. She glanced up at her mother and slowly lifted the lid. The first thing that caught Tessa's eye was a pair of faded ballet shoes. She held them up to her mother.

"Was Grandma a ballet dancer?" Tessa asked. She was surprised.

Her memory of Grandma was that she had used a stick to help her walk. It was hard to imagine Grandma dancing like she could.

"She was an amazing ballerina," Tessa's mother said with a sad smile. "Look in the box. It will explain everything."

"Well, that just reminds me that I can't dance." Tessa's
bad mood returned. She put the shoes down and
pretended she wasn't interested.

Tessa's mum stood up hurriedly.

"I've got work to do. You should look through the box
and then you'll get the whole story." And with that she
left Tessa alone.

Tessa settled back on the sofa. After a few minutes, she
grew curious. She wondered what else was in the box.
And she decided that she would like to see what was in
there, after all.

Tessa pulled out a black-and-white photograph of a beautiful ballerina. On the back of the photograph someone had written "Elizabeth, 16 April 1954. 16 years old."

"It's Grandma!" Tessa said to herself, surprised at how beautiful her grandma was.

She searched further through the box and found a pearl headpiece. It was the one Tessa's grandma was wearing in the photo.

Wow, thought Tessa.
These old things are so precious.

Tessa opened a crumpled old envelope addressed to her grandmother. Inside was a typed letter. Tessa could hardly believe what she was reading.

"No one ever told me that Grandma went to a famous ballet school."

22 July 1954

Dear Elizabeth,

It is with great pleasure that we accept you into The School of Ballet. You will start your program on 19 September.

We welcome you to our school and hope you find your time with us challenging and rewarding.

Yours sincerely,

Helene Di Monte

Tessa was excited to find out more. She pulled out an old newspaper article. It was about lots of people getting a new vaccination. This didn't interest Tessa so she folded it up and put it back in the box. She continued to look for more information about Grandma's ballet career.

At the bottom of the box she found Grandma's diary. She read the first page.

22 July 1955

One year ago, I received the most exciting letter of my life – my acceptance into The School of Ballet.

Little did I know that the best day of my life would soon turn into the worst day of my life. After opening the letter, I was so excited that I forgot I was feeling sick. My head ached, my throat was dry and my arms and legs felt stiff and sore.

My mother took me to the doctor.

"I think you have polio," the doctor said. "We will have to do some tests."

I was so scared. Surely this wasn't happening to me.

"Mum," called Tessa. "I need to ask you something."

"What is it?" Tessa's mum asked.

"Grandma wrote about having polio." Tessa looked up at her mum. "What's polio?"

"Oh," sighed Tessa's mum. "When Grandma was young, polio was a common disease. It made people very sick and some were left unable to walk."

"So that's why Grandma limped and needed a stick." Tessa was beginning to understand. "And was that why she stopped dancing?"

"She never danced again after that day," explained Tessa's mum.

"Oh, no!" responded Tessa with a lump in her throat.

Tessa's train of thought was interrupted by a knock at the door.

Her mum opened the door. "Tessa, guess who's here?"

"Molly!" Tessa's face lit up.

Molly settled next to Tessa on the sofa, where the two friends chatted and giggled. Tessa felt almost back to her old self.

Chapter 3

Tessa's bad news

Life was getting back to normal for Tessa. She was back at school and slowly getting better at using crutches. Some nights, she would read Grandma's diary and talk with her mum about it.

Three weeks after Tessa's accident, the doctor examined her ankle. "Your ankle isn't healing as quickly as I thought it would. You'll have to stay off it for another two weeks."

"Oh, no," said Tessa. "Can I dance at my concert?"

"We will have to wait and see," said the doctor.

"Two more weeks on these annoying crutches," grumbled Tessa, as she arrived home and slumped onto the sofa. As the bad news sank in, she was reminded of Grandma and her bad news. She pulled Grandma's diary out of the box and began to read.

5 November 1955

Today was difficult, but a big step. I went to the shops alone for the first time since I got sick. I am proud of myself, but I'm still very frustrated.

I struggle to get around on the crutches. Not long ago, I was strapped to a frame, unable to move at all.

This photo reminds me that I am lucky. Some people never recover from polio, so I'm doing okay.

Maybe two more weeks on these crutches won't be too bad after all, thought Tessa, as she turned the page.

This photo reminds me how glad I was when the doctor said I could try to learn to walk without the metal calipers.

Those calipers used to rub my legs and give me horrible blisters. They were noisy and heavy. I am so glad that I don't need them anymore.

I am lucky that I recovered, but I hate that I will never dance again.

Tessa was shocked at what she was reading. She put the diary down and looked out the window. Poor Grandma! she thought.

7 December 1955

Today was so hard. I'm doing lots of exercises on my weak legs and I am exhausted. But I think the exercises are working. I do feel a lot stronger.

I'm hoping that one day I will be able to walk using just a stick. Well, that's my goal. And I won't give up.

My dance days taught me to never give up. When I couldn't remember the steps to a routine, I would practise over and over and over until I got it.

That's what I need to do now.

Chapter 4

A decision for Tessa

Two weeks later, Tessa went back to the doctor. This time she received good news! And she couldn't wait to tell Molly. During the car ride home, she sent her a message.

Tessa 3:14PM

Guess what? I can dance again.

Molly 3:15PM

Wow! That's fantastic. I'm so excited.

Tessa 3:16PM

I know. Me too! The doctor said my ankle is much better. I don't even need crutches!

Molly 3:17PM

Can you dance in the concert?

Tessa 3:17PM

Hope so! xx

Molly 3:18PM

Awesome! :-)

The next day, Tessa returned to dance class. All the other dancers rushed to say hello as she appeared in the doorway of the dance studio.

"It's great to have you back, Tessa!" said Miss Mia.

Tessa smiled. She had missed dancing so much. She was so happy to be back doing what she loved.

"I do have some bad news though, Tessa." Miss Mia lowered her voice. "I'm sorry, but Molly is dancing the solo. You've just missed too many practices."

"I understand." Tessa was disappointed, but happy for her friend Molly. She smiled. "I'm just glad to be here at all."

"Okay everyone," Miss Mia said, organising the class. "The concert is next Saturday night. We need to make the most of our time. Here we go!"

The dancers rushed to their places. Tessa felt butterflies in her stomach. She was excited, but also nervous and her mind was racing – would her ankle be okay? Would she remember what to do after missing so many rehearsals?

That night after dance class, Tessa sat at home fighting back tears. She undid the tight bandage around her sore ankle and rubbed it gently. It wasn't the dull ache from her ankle that was upsetting her.

Her mum stopped what she was doing and looked at Tessa with concern. "What's the matter, Tessa? I thought you couldn't wait to get back to dancing."

"I was terrible, Mum," blurted out Tessa. "I kept making mistakes. I couldn't remember the routine. I'm going to make a fool of myself if I dance on Saturday."

"Oh, Tessa," said her mum. "You know you don't have to do the concert."

"Well, I'm not doing it!" said Tessa. "There's no way I'm dancing in the concert!"

Just then, a knock at the front door interrupted Tessa's outburst.

Tessa looked up as her mother led Miss Mia into the kitchen.

"Miss Mia," sniffed Tessa, hiding her tears. "What are you doing here?"

"I was worried about you," said Miss Mia. "You looked very nervous at rehearsal today. I'm just checking that you're feeling okay."

"I was hopeless," said Tessa. "I've made a decision. I'm not going to dance in the concert. I can't do it. It's just too hard."

"That's your decision, Tessa. If you change your mind, however, I'll go through the routine with you tomorrow after school. You'll have to do some extra practice between now and Saturday, but you'll be fine. You're a very good dancer."

"I used to be," said Tessa, "before I hurt my ankle."

"Just think about it," said Miss Mia.

"Okay," said Tessa. "But I won't change my mind."

That night Tessa couldn't sleep. She wished she could be happy with her decision not to dance, but something was worrying her.

And then she realised – Grandma. She felt so terribly sad for what her grandma had missed out on. Tessa realised that she had nothing to complain about compared to what her grandma had been through. Imagine getting a disease like polio and never being able to dance again. And that made Tessa wonder.

In the morning, she asked her mother why people don't get polio anymore.

"A vaccine was discovered!" said her mum. "You had the vaccine when you were a baby. Today, most people are vaccinated so they are protected from ever getting polio. What an important discovery that vaccine was!"

"That's what that old newspaper article was about," said Tessa. "Children getting the first polio vaccination."

She checked the date of the article – 13 April 1955. She checked Grandma's diary. Grandma was diagnosed with polio in 1954, the year before people were first vaccinated. She had only just missed out. How different her life could have been if she had been vaccinated, thought Tessa.

"I've decided to dance, Mum," said Tessa.

"I'm pleased that you've changed your mind," said her mum. She pulled the headpiece out of the box and smiled at Tessa. "You could wear Grandma's headpiece. I'm sure she'd like that."

"I'd like that, too," said Tessa.

Chapter 5

Dancing for Grandma

The night of the concert arrived. Tessa couldn't believe she was backstage with her friends getting ready to perform.

Tessa's breathing was rapid, her hands were sweaty and her heart was racing. What if she froze on stage? Why had she changed her mind? Why had she decided to do the concert?

But it was too late to back out now. Tessa took some slow, deep breaths. She checked in the mirror that the headpiece was in place.

"I'm dancing for you tonight, Grandma." Tessa spoke the words in a whisper as she moved into position.

The lights dimmed. The curtain rose. The music started. And the dancers performed!

Before Tessa knew it, the concert was over. The audience clapped and cheered.

I think I was all right, thought Tessa.

"You did it, everyone!" cried Miss Mia. "You were all magnificent!"

The dancers jumped around excitedly. Tessa smiled proudly. All her extra work had paid off.

Tessa's mum came backstage and hugged Tessa tightly.

"I knew you could do it. Grandma would have been so proud of you. You were wonderful!"

Miss Mia embraced her, too. "Tessa, I'm so proud of you for dancing tonight. I know it was hard. You're so very, very brave!"

Tessa smiled and her hand moved to her headpiece. A small voice in her head was telling her that Grandma would have been proud of her.

"I'm not brave, Miss Mia," she said. "I'm lucky!"

"What do you mean?" asked Miss Mia.

"I'm lucky because I got the chance to dance again," said Tessa. "Not everyone gets a second chance to do the things they love."

A note from the author

I remember when I was about ten I missed a basketball final because I wasn't well. I was devastated! My team won and I was happy for them, but I felt sorry for myself. I remembered this incident as I was writing about Tessa's feelings when she hurt her ankle and was in danger of missing her concert.

I included the diary written by Tessa's grandma in this story because I felt it was a good way to directly hear from someone who had been through the tragedy of having polio. When I was younger, my father came across an audio recording of my great uncle who had died about ten years earlier. The recording was so interesting. My great uncle spoke about his life and how difficult his childhood had been. Hearing this made me feel very lucky about how easy my childhood had been. This was in the back of my mind as I wrote about Tessa's reactions to reading her grandma's diary.